Breath Prayers for Anxiety

Whispers of *Prayer*

Julie Kay Harbour

Book Cover by Julie Kay Harbour
Page Design by Julie Kay Harbour

Other books by Julie Kay Harbour:

Biblical Journaling for
Anxiety

Biblical Journaling for
Finding Your Identity In Christ

Biblical Journaling for
Renewing Your Mind

Dear Reader,

Thank you for picking up this book of breath prayers. My hope is that as you turn each page, you'll find peace, strength, and renewed closeness with God. Life has a way of making our hearts race and our minds feel overwhelmed, but in the quiet moments of breathing, we can refocus on the One who gives us life and sustains us.

This book was created to offer you a way to calm your mind, center your heart, and reconnect with the deep, abiding presence of God. The prayers you'll find here are simple yet powerful. Each one is designed to help you pause, breathe deeply, and rest in God's Word. The rhyming format is meant to help these prayers stay with you throughout the day, becoming a rhythm of peace for your soul.

Breath prayers are more than just a spiritual practice. They bring physical, emotional, and spiritual benefits. Taking time to breathe deeply calms the nervous system, reduces stress, and invites God into those moments of stillness. It allows us to align our hearts with His, to lay down our burdens, and to remember that He is in control.

I encourage you to take this journey slowly. Whether you're using these prayers to begin your day, a pause in a busy moment, or winding down at night, know that each breath you take is a gift from God, and each prayer is an opportunity to draw closer to Him. Let this be your invitation to breathe in His grace and exhale your worries.

May this book bless you as you create space for God's peace, and may prayer become a part of your everyday rhythm, renewing your heart and mind with the breath of life.

Warmly and Sincerely,

Julie Kay

"Do not conform to the pattern of this world, but be transformed by the renewing of your m Then you will be able to test and approve what God's will is—his good, pleasing and perfec

JUST breathe

"Be still and know that I am God."

Psalm 46:10 , ESV

How to Engage in a Breath Prayer

❋ Slowly take in a deep, full breath breathing in through your nose.

❋ With your lungs full, hold the air in your lungs while saying the the first line of the breath prayer.

❋ Slowly exhale, releasing the air through pursed lips.

❋ After you exhale, say the last line of the breath prayer.

(It's important to ensure you breathe from your diaphragm, not your chest. One way to do this is to place one hand on your upper abdomen and the other on your chest. As you breathe in and out, the hand on your abdomen should rise and fall with each breath, not the hand on your chest.)

Draw near to God and He will draw near to you.

James 4:8a, ESV

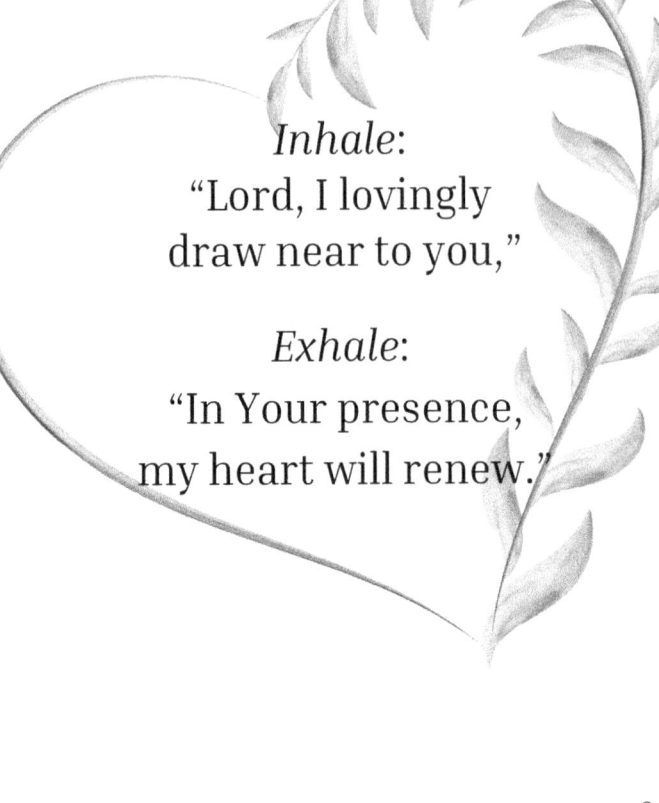

Inhale:
"Lord, I lovingly
draw near to you,"

Exhale:
"In Your presence,
my heart will renew."

When I am

afraid

I put my

trust in you.

Psalm 56:3, ESV

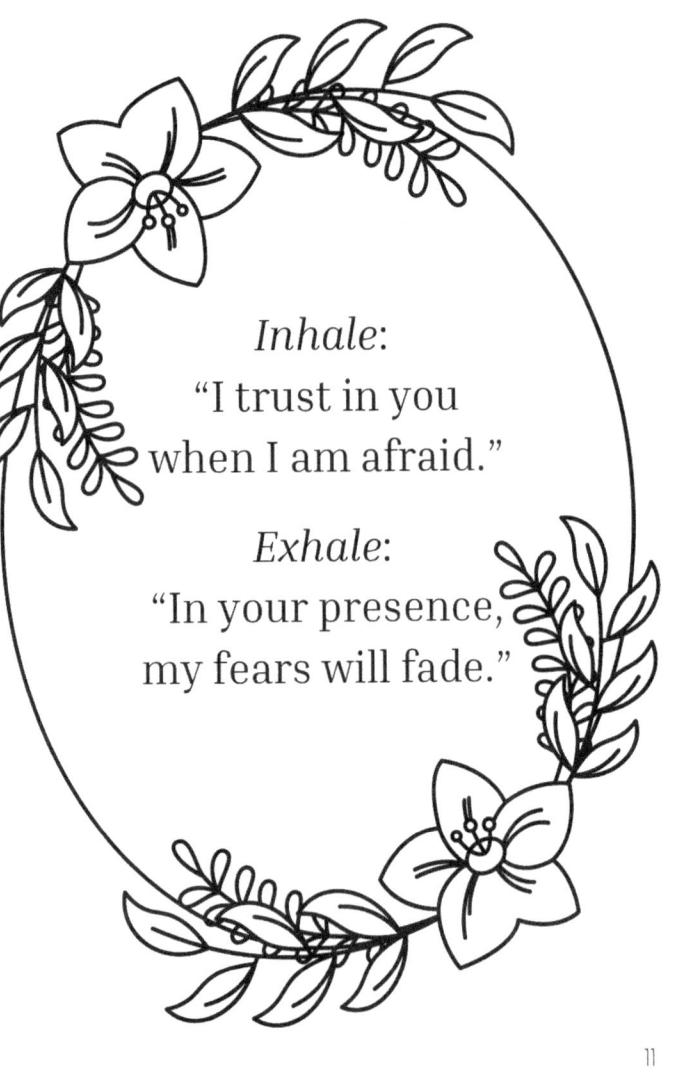

Inhale:
"I trust in you
when I am afraid."

Exhale:
"In your presence,
my fears will fade."

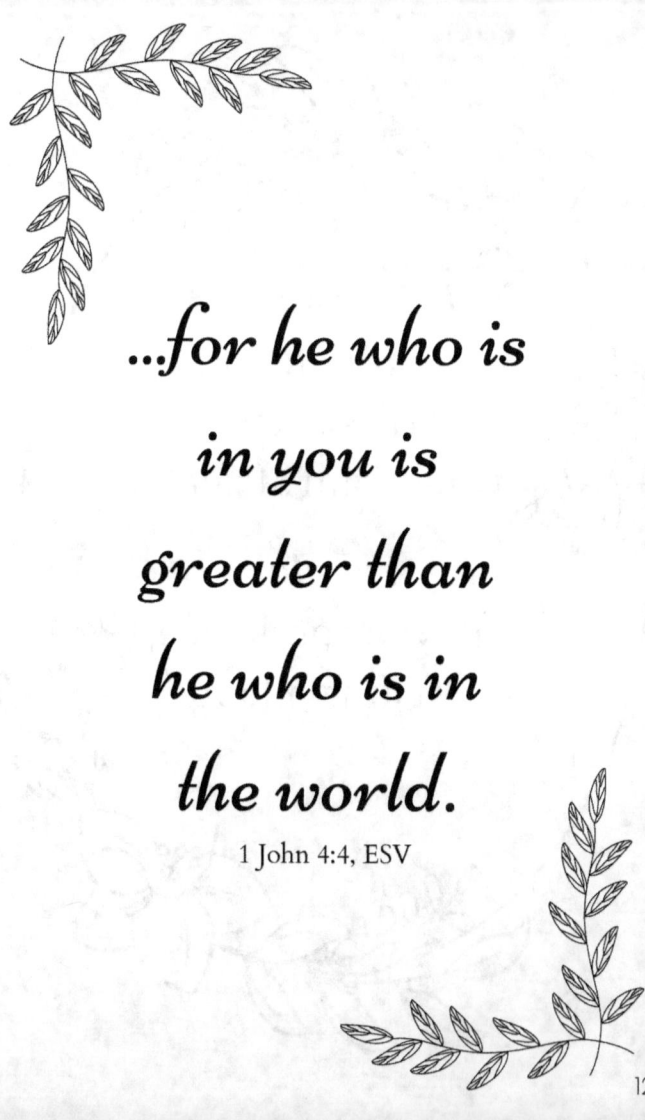

...for he who is
in you is
greater than
he who is in
the world.

1 John 4:4, ESV

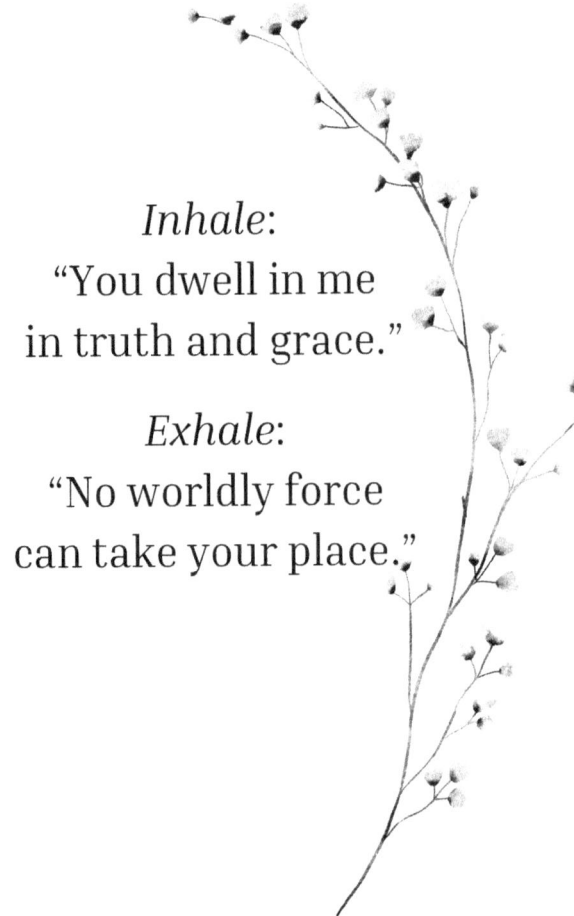

Inhale:
"You dwell in me
in truth and grace."

Exhale:
"No worldly force
can take your place."

You keep track
of all my sorrows
You have collected
all my tears
in your bottle.
You have recorded
each one in
your book.

Psalm 56:8, NLT

Inhale:
"You hold my tears
with tender care."

Exhale:
"Within your love,
I find repair."

For God has not given me a spirit of fear, but of power, and love and of a sound mind.

2 Timothy 1:7, NKJV

Inhale:
"No spirit of fear,
but power,"

Exhale:
"Your love and peace
every hour."

He makes me
lie down in
green pastures,
he leads me
beside still waters.
He restores
my soul.

Psalm 23:2-3, ESV

Inhale:
"In green pastures,
You restore."

Exhale:
"Lead me, Lord,
forevermore."

Cast your

anxiety on him

for he cares

for you.

1 Peter 5:7, NIV

Inhale:
"I cast my cares
into your hands."

Exhale:
"Your peace with me
forever stands."

Don't worry about anything; instead pray about everything. Tell God what you need and thank him for all he has done. Then you will experience God's peace which exceeds anything we can understand.

Phil. 4:6 NLT

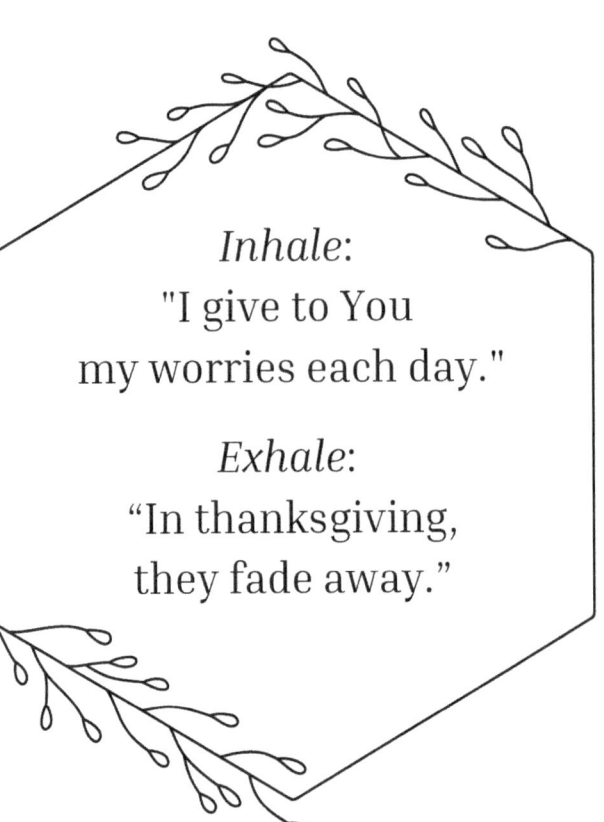

Inhale:
"I give to You
my worries each day."

Exhale:
"In thanksgiving,
they fade away."

Trust in him at all times, you people; pour out your hearts to him, for God is our refuge.

Psalm 62:8 NIV

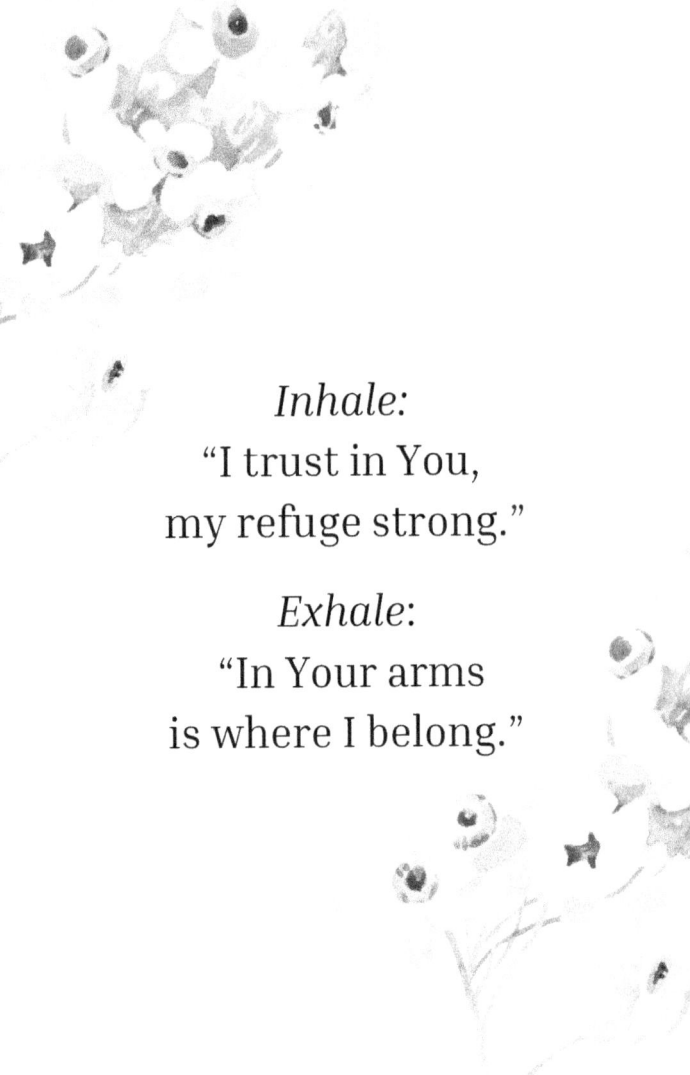

Inhale:
"I trust in You,
my refuge strong."

Exhale:
"In Your arms
is where I belong."

The Lord himself
goes before you
and will be with you;
he will never
leave you
nor forsake you.
Do not be afraid;
do not be
discouraged.

Deut. 31:8 NIV

Inhale:
"You go before me,
and still, you're near."

Exhale:
"Because you're with me,
I will not fear."

Trust in the Lord with all your heart, and lean not on your own understanding. In all your ways acknowledge Him and He shall direct your paths.

Prov. 3:5-6 NKJV

Inhale:
"I trust in You
with all my heart."

Exhale:
"Direct my path;
I will not part."

I can do all things through Christ who strengthens me.

Phil 4:13 NKJV

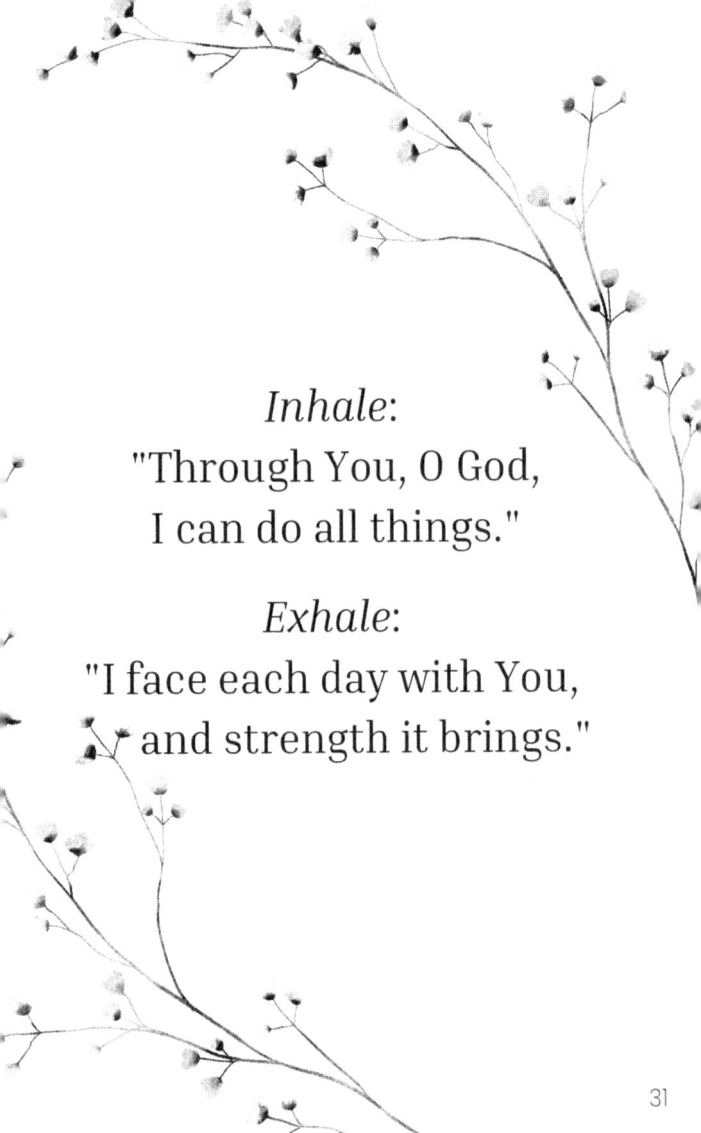

Inhale:
"Through You, O God,
I can do all things."

Exhale:
"I face each day with You,
and strength it brings."

Surely your goodness and love will follow me all the days of my life, and I will dwell in the house of the Lord forever.

Psalm 23:6 NIV

Inhale:
"Your goodness
and love follow me."

Exhale:
"In Your house,
I will always be."

You will keep me in perfect peace those whose minds are steadfast, because they trust in you.

Isaiah 26:3-4 NIV

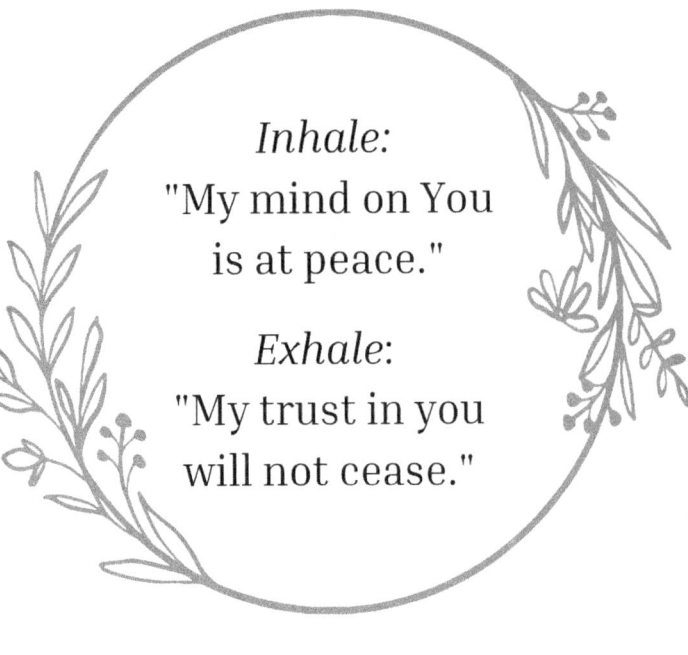

Inhale:
"My mind on You
is at peace."

Exhale:
"My trust in you
will not cease."

Have I not
commanded you?
Be strong and
courageous.
Do not be afraid;
do not be discouraged,
for the Lord your God
will be with you
wherever you go.
Joshua 1:9 NIV

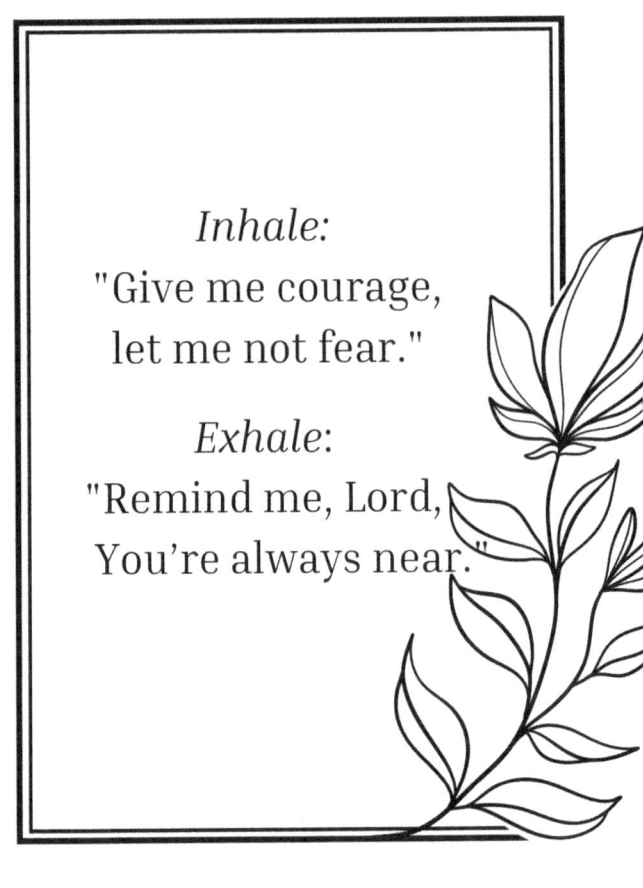

Inhale:
"Give me courage,
let me not fear."

Exhale:
"Remind me, Lord,
You're always near."

And we know that in all things God works for the good of those who love him, who have been called according to his purpose.

Romans 8:28, NIV

Inhale:
"You work all things
for my good."

Exhale:
"Help me trust You
as I should."

Then they cried out to the Lord in their trouble, and he brought them out of their distress. He stilled the storm to a whisper, the waves of the sea were hushed.

Psalm 107:28-29, NIV

Inhale:
"Hush, my storm,
Oh God, bring peace."

Exhale:
"Into Your hands,
my fears I release."

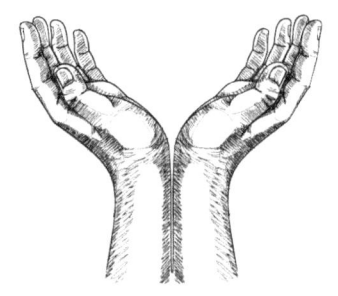

I have told you
these things,
so that in me you
may have peace.
In this world you
will have trouble.
But take heart!
I have overcome
the world.

John 16:33, NIV

Inhale:
"In this world,
I will find trouble."

Exhale:
"But, your peace, Lord,
is more than double."

...Do not fear, for I have redeemed you; I have summoned you by name; you are mine. When you pass through the waters, I will be with you; and when you pass through the rivers, they will not sweep over you. When you walk through the fire, you will not be burned; the flames will not set you ablaze.

Isaiah 43:1-2, NIV

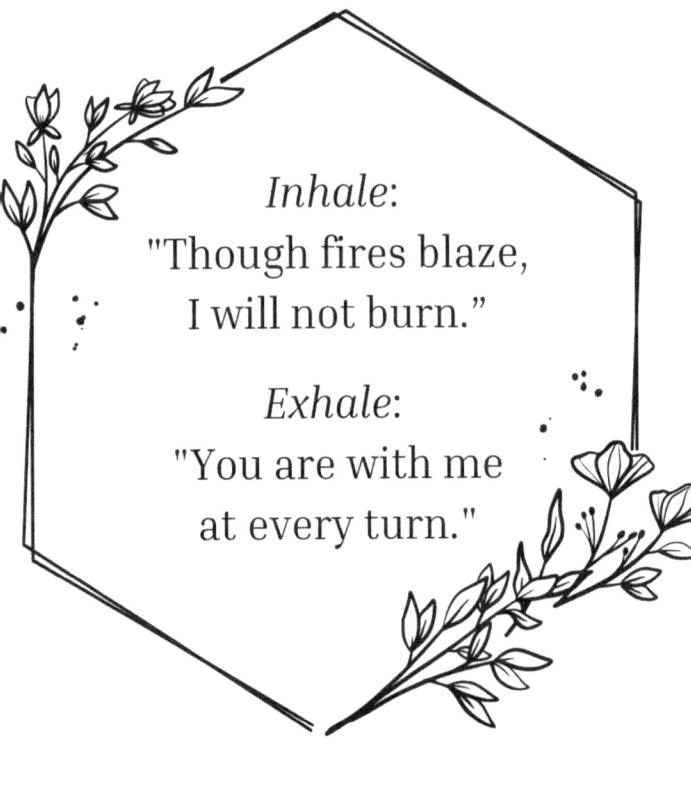

Inhale:
"Though fires blaze,
I will not burn."

Exhale:
"You are with me
at every turn."

From the end of
the earth I will
cry to You,
When my heart is
overwhelmed;
Lead me to the
rock that is
higher than I.

Psalm 61:2, NKJV

Inhale:
"From the ends of the earth,
to You, I cry."

Exhale:
"Lead me to Your
refuge on high."

Peace I leave
with you;
my peace I give you.
I do not give to you
as the world gives.
Do not let your hearts
be troubled and
do not be afraid.

John 14:27, NIV

Inhale:
"Fill my heart with peace
not fear."

Exhale:
"Your perfect love
is always near."

...Though I have
fallen, I will rise.
Though I sit
in darkness,
the Lord will
be my light.

Micah 7:8, NIV

Inhale:
"When I fall,
lift me to you,"

Exhale:
"Shine Your light,
and guide me through."

Then Christ will
make his home
in your hearts as
you trust in him.
Your roots will
grow down into
God's love and
keep you strong.

Eph. 3:17, NLT

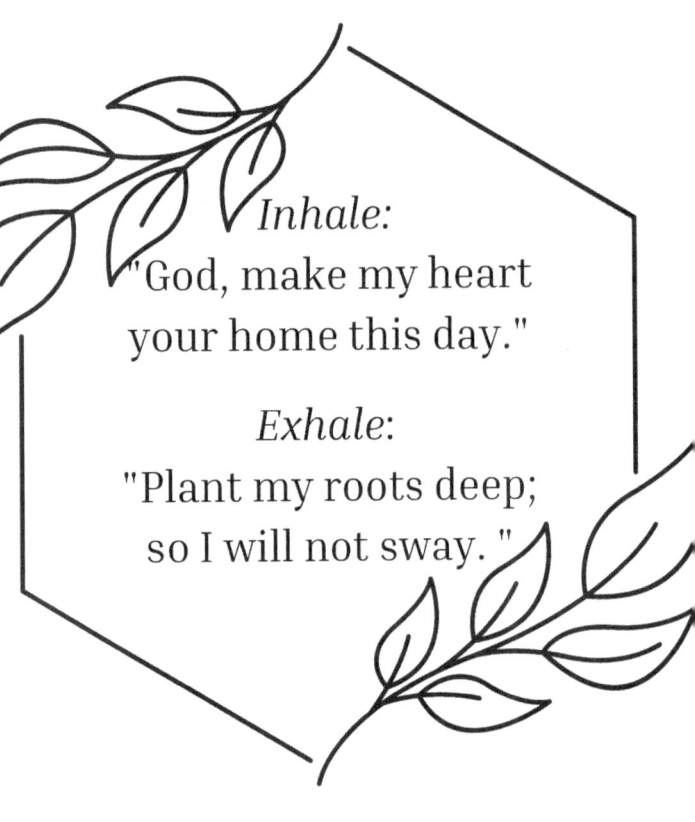

Inhale:
"God, make my heart
your home this day."

Exhale:
"Plant my roots deep;
so I will not sway. "

He will cover you
with his feathers.
He will shelter you
with his wings.
His faithful promises
are your armor
and protection.

Psalm 91:4, NLT

Inhale:
"Cover me with
Your wings so wide."

Exhale:
"In Your promises,
I will abide."

Don't be afraid for
I am with you.
Don't be discouraged
for I am your God.
I will strengthen
you and help you.
I will hold you
with my victorious
right hand.

Isaiah 41:10, NLT

Inhale:
"No harm against me
will ever stand."

Exhale:
"You hold me up with your
righteous hand."

I lift my eyes up to the mountains - where does my help come from? My help comes from the Lord, the Maker of heaven and earth.

Psalm 12:1-2, NIV

Inhale:
"Up to the mountains,
I lift my eyes."

Exhale:
"You are my Help,
My Maker, my Prize."

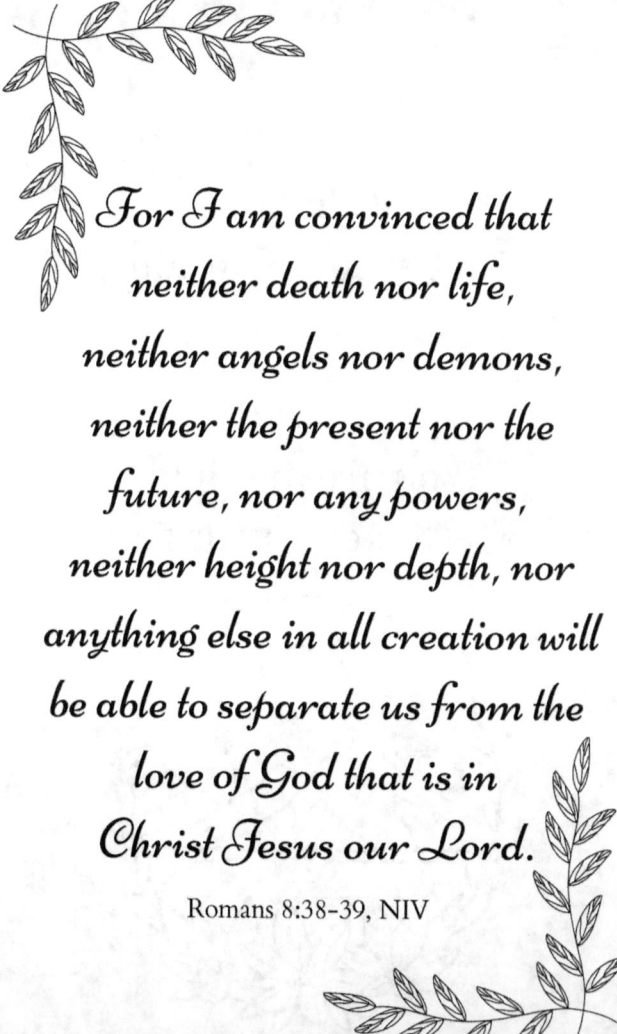

For I am convinced that neither death nor life, neither angels nor demons, neither the present nor the future, nor any powers, neither height nor depth, nor anything else in all creation will be able to separate us from the love of God that is in Christ Jesus our Lord.

Romans 8:38–39, NIV

Inhale:
"Of all that is,
you rise above."

Exhale:
"Nothing separates me
from your love."

Let us hold unswervingly to the hope we profess, for he who promised is faithful.

Hebrews 10:23, NIV

Inhale:
"Holding on to the hope
that I profess."

Exhale:
"Your love, truth,
and grace
I will confess."

Come to me, all you who are weary and carry heavy burdens, and I will give you rest. Let me teach you, because I am humble and gentle at heart, and you will find rest for your souls.

Matthew 11:28-29, NLT

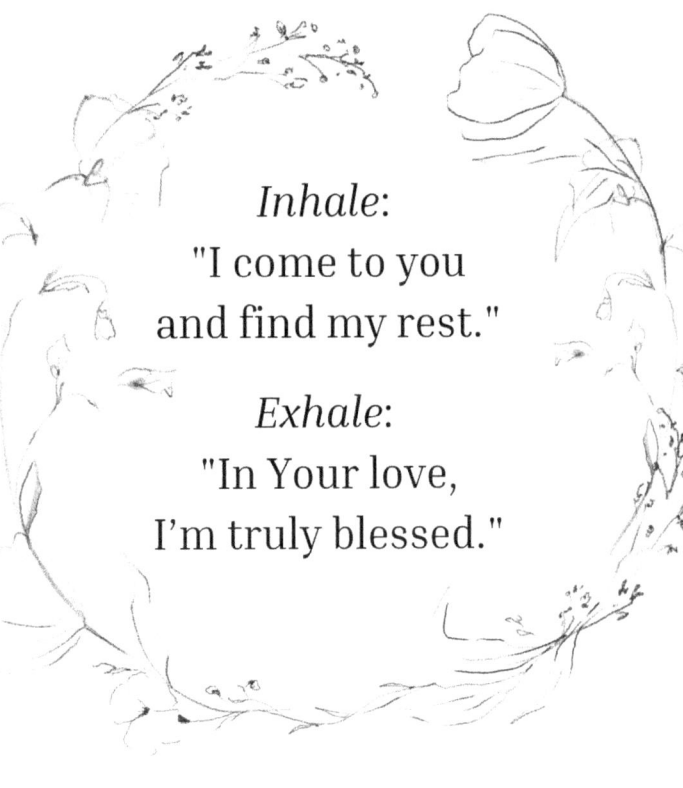

Inhale:
"I come to you
and find my rest."

Exhale:
"In Your love,
I'm truly blessed."

For no word from God will ever fail.

Luke 1:37, NIV

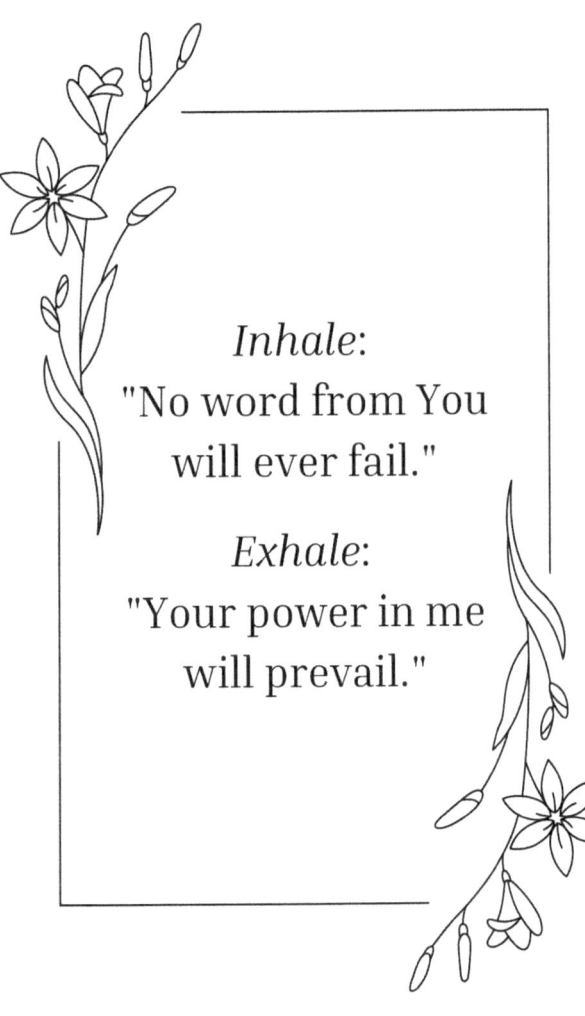

Inhale:
"No word from You
will ever fail."

Exhale:
"Your power in me
will prevail."

ABOUT THE AUTHOR

Julie Kay Harbour, a native Texan, brings a wealth of diverse experiences to her work and is deeply committed to helping others grow spiritually. Raised in a Christian home, she attended the Methodist Church with her family before transitioning to the Baptist Church as a teenager, and now she attends a non-denominational church. Julie holds a Bachelor of Science in Elementary Education from Baylor University and an MBA from TCU, both in Texas. Additionally, she is a Certified Natural Health Professional (CNHP), a certification pursued due to the health challenges she and her son have faced.

Julie is the creator of the Biblical Journaling method and the founder of JK Creations. Her background and experiences have fueled her fascination with the human brain and its extraordinary capabilities, a passion that is evident throughout her writing and work. Family is central to Julie's life; being the only female in her household, which consists of her husband and two teenage boys, has fostered a deep appreciation for female companionship and meaningful connections.

When she's not caring for her family or tending to her yard, she finds joy in nature, science, art, music, and all things creative. Her prayer is that God will guide her to use her strengths and gifts to encourage and meet the needs of others.

Julie Kay Harbour

JK Creations crafts inspired writing and innovative products rooted in Philippians 4:8, celebrating what is true, noble, right, pure, lovely, admirable, excellent, and praiseworthy. Through thoughtful words and design, we inspire and equip others to align their thinking with God's truth.

Thank you for reading Whispers of Prayer: Breath Prayers for Anxiety. I would love to stay connected with you!

🌐 Visit my website:
www.juliekayharbour.com

📘 Follow me on Facebook:
www.facebook.com/juliekayharbour

📷 Follow me on Instagram:
www.instagram.com/juliekayharbour

📩 Are you wanting more inspiration and encouragement? Sign up for my newsletter, "Helping You to Renew", by subscribing on my website. Receive inspiration, tips, updates, and more ways to renew your mind.

Let's continue this journey together!